My Eternal Truths

By: Jessica Brown

Made with ❤ on the BookLeaf Publishing Platform
www.bookleafpub.in
www.bookleafpub.com

Dedication

I dedicate this creation to the FATHER above
Thank you for your presence through it all

Preface

These poems entail the life I continuously try my best to
live.
These poems were all created after a time where I
allowed God to curate my views on many situations in
my life.
God comes first in my life and love comes from Him so
that I can share it with all of those around me.
These poems portray the times after I hit rock bottom
and realized God was the rock I needed to build my
foundation on.
So please enjoy reading my love for God, my family &
expression.

Acknowledgements

Where would I be without my support system?
God is my priority; the one that keeps me focused.
My family is a reminder of why I must grow.
My partner is a thought provoker who takes me outside
my shell.
My therapist is a cheerleader who said I should write a
book & look where we are.
My community in general is who pushes me to continue
on this beautiful journey with GOD.
And finally, my inner child is who seeks true creative
freedom.

Prayer

Dear Reader,

I thank you for being here. I am grateful for your presence as well as your eyes & minds being able to read these pages. I pray that these works & wonders of GOD reach your heart, mind, & spirit. I pray that these poems meet you where you are & propel you forward on your journey with The ALMIGHTY. Thank you again!
ALL GLORY TO GOD! Amen<3

GOD SPEAKS

trust God's sense of direction
there's power within his breeze

any sense of doubt
find humor in its entirety

flow like water; not knowing
sway in time while growing

your path is light
peace guides you through

the story you're sticking to, it's about you
no one else knows your view

you may share, and they may care
answers are within your core, not theirs

your path is illuminated
walk it with strength, faith, & courage

remember pain is temporary
your health equals your abundance

breathe through so you can see through
what's holding you back is a cloud

as long as your sense of direction is God
held; you will prevail

definition is infinite
mold yours around more than just existing

strain is the pathway to gain
temporarily; it'll move out of the way

Yahweh is the divine creator & planner
Allow Him to lead you, sinner

GOD PREPARES MY WAY

I love what God has gifted me
the glory to just be
in his presence of love, light, and peace
In this season, God is the present I need
a blessing I now know of & hold dearly
see, there is no such thing as insecurity
but only clarity
In my mind, everyone is beautiful
even me, there's no other way to be
God's image is the painting
what's meant to be will be
that's what I tell myself
it's what I truly believe
a path previously laid out for me to follow
God's blessing & guidance laid upon me
my eyes fill with water as I wander
fully putting my all into God
nowhere near easy; the only way to be
reaching only out to Him
His hand is my ladder to climb onto

I question my ability as if I don't know me
but I know everything there is to know
no one has been in my shoes or my hair
still, they stare as if they know everything
I'm scared to go alone but what's new
I've received my clues
letting God curate my views
guiding me to make the right moves
His path is my truth
there is no other way through
Don't be scared, God is near
pointing you in the right direction
follow Him, he knows all there is to know
fear of anything else is desolate
but fear of God is heaven-sent
don't forget what you felt
keep it under your belt
allow it to propel you forward
it's why you surrendered
the first step is acknowledgment; remember
God allow me to see the light
allow me to trust its might
as I cry at night, yes I'm tired
but I know I must fight
I must walk through to grow through

BRING GOD IN

God has shown me many times
I could die any day
but still, I rot and fill my heart with dismay
I should be welcoming him into my life
willingly & open-heartedly
I've surrendered before
why is it so hard now that it's finally 2024
a new year has elapsed
but still, here I am fighting with the air
I breathe and the devil tries to come in
I seek and the devil tries again
but God he sees me, feels me, & seeks me
as I do him
it's just I feel hopeless as if I'm caving in
into the hole of the unknown
a space I once trusted
a place I now know nothing about
but isn't that the point; to know nothing
know nothing of what's coming out
the outcome is invisible like the journey

there's beauty in it's love for me
the unknown's desire to chase glory
the unknown's glory to seek peace
helping me not only seek but soon see
past the pain and heartache
but to the end of turmoil
& beginning of: letting go & receiving peace

LET GOD BE GOD

I can lead someone to the plan
but I'm not the planner
I can lead someone to help
but I'm not the helper
I can lead someone to the resources
but I'm not the source
I can lead someone to GOD
but I'm not GOD
I can't implement GOD in their life
I can't build their faith
but I can display the works of GOD
what he does
what he seeks
what he values
to be true & coming from HIS view
I know what I can do & what I can't do
GOD will guide you where you're meant to be
Don't worry about anyone else's journey
If they're meant to be gifted by GOD
he will make a way for them to be near

GOD will gift their present when they learn to be in HIS
presence
leave it up to them to build their faith in GOD
GOD will carry them
it's not for me to be their provider, seeker, or teacher
GOD will give them the necessary tools for what HE
asks them to do
You can display what it looks like to be with GOD
but you can't force them to experience what it means to
be with the LORD

WHAT GOD CAN DO

what once was desolate, even nonexistent
is now curated & heaven-sent
GOD created these unimaginable wonders
no man can replicate
Only GOD can delegate
such an acquired aftermath & outcome
your past doesn't define you
trust it, especially under the views of GOD
He is the one who created you
Just think of the people of Nazareth
so jealous & offended by JESUS' uprising
some people are so attached to your past
they can't have belief in your future
don't let others' views be yours too
you will receive what you're meant to
you'll also release
what was never meant to be a part of you
with GOD, all is possible
those addictions & narratives
even what's deemed socially imperative

don't doubt GOD'S ability
due to man's inability

STEPS = CORE 1234

I don't want to have to worry about
food on my plate
clothes on my back
rent being paid

not enough
strength
money
stability of foundation

they all need a sense of
concentration
dedication
attention

all this focus on winning; but when
all this life to live
all this love to give
but when will I gain & destroy the pain

Putting in the work but
doubting each step of the way
not fulfilled with my plate
no designated pathway

just being to be
not to be is not a choice
existing is my cup of tea
haven't had it in a while, but it's necessary

1 2 3 4
this progression is within your core
these stanzas are stairs to your future
all the answers you've been waiting for

searching within
this is the path you walk to heal
each step is a score towards inner work
temperance necessary for deliverance

the lack has led you to your mission
the question used to be what & why
now you know where God has led you
it's now up to you to turn the page

yes pain was once your sub-story
but you've worked your way to eliminate

that part was just the process of progress
climbing the ladder is now the only way

discovery is your journey
passion is your mission
in all aspects, growth is your strength
transformation is no longer your storm

it's what keeps you warm
involvement of mind, body, & soul
God has led you to bud
it's up to you to continue to transform

DO YOUR BEST & REST

find tranquility in every moment
each step has peace in its sway
don't let chaos tread on your thoughts
let it go as love & light transpire
your journey is yours to enjoy
show God gratitude through your views
perspective is key to tranquility
let silence be your solace
let light be your guidance
the flow ahead is meant for your rebirth
it may seem surreal
but only a step, in reality, shows you the depth
your circumstances will give you a stance
redirection is now your slow dance
transformation is the gift that keeps giving
no matter how ill or real, life will heal
every question will have an answer
never worry my friends
God is holding your hand
prayers for you wishing you the best

angels & ancestors watch over
as you take your next steps...

UNCERTAINTY BUT TRUSTING

in & out

ebb & flow

Yin & Yang

life & death

illumination & darkness

balance in this mess we call the world

land; still & grounding

ocean; uncertain & flowing

uprooted & swayed

a life we live every day

walking a path we know nothing about

but trusting that it's the right one anyway

the pain of the past still lingers

but as we flow, the past is let go

healing isn't a destination

to heal is to feel & be a part of the journey

the unknown keeps it real

letting us know that we can't control

even if everything feels surreal

it's okay to have faith & be within
within the bounds of mind, body, & soul
motion of emotion; a part making us whole
having faith isn't easy
it wasn't meant to be
those that can go through and grow without holding on
choose to flow
with The One we call GOD
HE brings upon us a heart of peace
learning how to love & be free
knowing we experience grief
GOD still guides the movement of our feet
it's up to us to trust HIS mastery
although our path is a mystery
YAHWEH's path leads to victory

DELIVERY

Give it to GOD, HE will provide every time
GOD will handle it, you will prevail in it
HIS guidance is heaven-sent
GOD's with you, it's guaranteed
HIS love is all that's necessary
HE'S guiding you to peace
Expect nothing from man
GOD will carry you through
Guided by HIS gentle hand & plan for you

GRADUAL LOVE

In my journey of love
what's necessary for me
continues changing & evolving
what I needed then
versus what I need now
Two completely different things
I need emotional availability
instead of attachment & emptiness
I'm in a space of needing fulfillment
in many ways than one
As I'm learning what's necessary
I'm also learning what's temporary
what grounds me & gives me peace
instead of the disease of momentary pleasure
Finding love within everything
instead of one person, place, or thing
As my journey within love continues to be a
mystery, I'm remembering to
love me unconditionally
If no one else will, that becomes my mission

to love within as I live without
within everything I'm here for me
& without anything, I'm still here for me
Just as GOD is
HE'S teaching me many things
leaning me towards HIS plans for me
I answer to HIM
not others or to my flesh
After many adversities, He's teaching me
to love still but differently this time around
How I must love still but from a distance
How I must love still but not forgetting
Learning to love difficult people differently
at first, it was all misery & sabotage
now it's me learning to love still
unconditionally within difficulty
being at a distance is better than being
disrespected & distracted from my path
GOD is giving me a new heart
HE is making me a new person
allowing me to see through other points of view
allowing his way of love to flow through
HIS love is why I pray for you
near or far, you're in my prayers
praying you learn to love like GOD wants you to
a love that's slowly, but surely progressing
allowing you to know what it means to lean on GOD

allowing you to give & receive
allowing you to love yourself & others willingly

LOVE IS A JOURNEY

Maya Angelou once said Love liberates
to me, love does not just set you free
it allows you to see things differently
shift within another perspective
understand that love is all around you
not within just one person place or thing
receive the love, give the love, see the love
understand that love is beauty and sometimes love is
pain but after each lost love there's no blessing in vain
confide in seeing that love is change
transformation is love that Metamorphisizes from pain
Love is within me
it divinely protects me
it's allows me to live after every adversity or difficulty
love is healing me internally & externally
Love is understanding that you can turn pain into power
And devour any darkness that tried to hover around you
like a coward
My superpower is loving every aspect of every person &
everything without controlling

Love allows me to love myself inside and out
Love is growth
Love is power
Love is energy
Love is manifesting all around even within those dark
roaming clouds
Love is many things, but to me, love is my destiny
will love set you free or will love exist only in a world
filled with negativity

LOVE IS REQUIRED

love always
they say
Love anyway even after the pain
let love liberate
set you free within the depths of your reality
love speaks to me
love guides my body
love induces my sexuality; my fluidity
love is like a tree flowing in every means of our destiny
Love is within me
love is within you too if you just grab onto the view
love gotcha like love got me too
be within that perspective to know that love is all around
even in those dark roaming clouds
you gotta know that love is our truth
truthfully speaking love is how I see you eliminating that
negativity that tries to creep through
my intuition let me know that love is the way I move for
growth to migrate too
that's why I love always

love is the answer to my whys
love is real wise when you allow it to flow through time
love heals parts of you
connects you to the Divine
love is the eyes for those lies you can't see through
love is how you open up to see behind the illusions
beneath you
let love guide you, protect you, support you
let love be you
in a world of darkness be the light
love is the illumination we all need
love fills my cup of tea
you see love flows through us like the waves of the sea
love is my eve
in other words, love is my way of living

LOVE ALWAYS

My experiences taught me to Love Always
even if the outcome is pain
allow your heart to be open for love to stay
you may be rewarded for your ways
you may not be but that's okay
love is the answer that we're searching for
it's within our core
some may say love is blowing in the wind
but when are we going to recognize that love is always
within
love is the help we need for ourselves & the betterment
of the world around us
love is the truth within all the trauma we've conditioned
ourselves to
love always & you will be rewarded in your days for
trying to make the world a better place
L O V E is how we see through the constructed lenses of
society
you have a choice to love or hate

love is my way & I hope I can encourage you to make
every day a love day

MY SWEET BUTTERFLY

My sweet butterfly
shines so bright
that's her light
so divine
one-of-a-kind
she's all mine
my sweet butterfly
born from christ
seeks her truth
grows on through
dreams so high
right time
slow down vibes
all the time
my sweet butterfly
frequency guides
through the night
a beautiful mind
that's my nana
by my side

even when I have no clue
an everlasting butterfly
guided by GOD'S gentle hand

FATHER

I'm glad I did what I did
Now I can build the type of relationship I always wanted
then
Letting go of you and opening the door for someone new
Someone better. Someone who cares for me. Someone
who loves me unconditionally.
Someone who doesn't judge the me that I'm becoming.
Someone who checks on me without overthinking
I love this person truly.
You blocked the love I was able to give but now I've
completely forgotten you so you no longer impact the
way I live.
I forgive & I forget.
Now on to the next cycle of my life that's better for me &
for some of the people around me.
Thanks, J for showing me that you want to stay and
putting actions over words.
Any day.
Another rebirth.
A better rebirth.

A new transformation within the love around me.
Just for you.
New idealization of the newfound figure that grew.
I'm so proud of letting myself acknowledge that there
could be good within the bad perceptions of father
figures from my past
the ones I never really knew
Now there's you
Someone I can finally open up to
without feeling a lack of trust
that was the issue then
I continued to give
even if it hurt
now realizing the red flags firsthand
now cutting off all people like that so the past can no
longer linger within
But thank you again for the old that brought in the new.
balance of turning pain into power
devouring the darkness & showering the light
embracing the times I had to fight
because they're what illuminated me to the right
pathway that I was always meant to be on
recognizes the universe's power was always okay to lean
on
the things they did for me to grow.
Thank you past, I now let you go with love & light
within my mind, body, & soul!

A closed chapter
support now coming from the above
You stuck it through and helped me live
as you fulfilled every part of your destiny
intuitively guiding me to heal parts of myself I didn't
want to feel
Thank J, you always kept it real

WITHOUT FOR NOW

every time I think of you
I cry at the thought of no longer seeing you when I want
to
no longer being able to call
or sharing moments with you
I miss you
a day gone by
turns to weeks
to months
to years without you near me
time is no longer the same
without you in my space, I hardly know what's real &
what's fake
03:01 on the clock
I reminisce & ponder in my thoughts
can't seem to remember every little moment
I think I honestly forgot
But still, even though your absence is surreal
I know GOD'S presence is keeping me still
stable in what I was able to feel when you were here &

grounded in your love that helped me heal

35

MOTHER

If she can do it so can we; destiny
change is a difficult thing
one thing about my mom; she's adapting
she's gone through many adversities
not once did she give up
she allowed GOD to push her through
did she make mistakes along the way
yes, but change & forgiveness is key
each step taken is gradually shaking
crumbling old foundations once built
creating new; it's never too late
give GOD your plate
the one that overwhelms with dismay
never did appreciate the taste
but she pushed through anyway
unknowingly changing her ways
transformation swaying into fruition
Thank GOD for giving her permission
allowing her to grow & become herself
even if she's learning or asking for help

my mom has life underneath her belt
the beauty within getting older
newfound maturity in my mother
how could I not love her
the one who took care of me
the one who reminded me of my beauty
the one who fought to keep me safe
no, I can't forget
the other emotions she put into motion
but I can forgive
as we're growing a new connection within
distance is put between us
but new moments are being captured
ones I'll always remember
I hope as my mom looks in the mirror
she sees the storms she's gotten through
with or without me or you
GOD has been leading her here
to a better spiritual view
life isn't perfect in any room
but since then she's gained a new sense
Listening to her FATHER
obedience leading her the right way
YAHWEH is great
allowing me to love more than ever
before my mind was troubled
making me hate due to our surroundings

but as I grow, I'm learning to know
know that control isn't our own
GOD guides us where we're meant to be
no matter the amount of misery
or lessons learned
HE leads us to our greatest victories
mentally, physically & spiritually
GOD seeks progression in imperfection

INFINITELY TREASURED

the love I share with one kind soul
our paths have crossed to meet
the middle, where we are grounded even if we're far
I hold his hand in gratitude
in grace, the shadow is left behind
he's mine as I am his
our love in the air whispers only for us to hear
it flows as our souls fly on
together I'm glad to be
seeing his smile brings about a beautiful tranquil breeze
this way of life that'll never cease
I wish, I pray, I say with the love in my heart, I hope it's
you forever
you treat me as you would a woman
but you love me as you know to love
it's your bubbly way I hope will stay
your tenderness brings peace
transformation seeps along our feet like sand
I'm glad to be your friend & your romance
your heart touches mine as your arms lace around my

body hugging me tightly
we both share the light of the day
my sun to your moon
stars are aligned as we meet eye-to-eye
I cry wishing to hold on for life
to grow as one
souls connected and free at the same time
I strive to continue to grow within myself but also with
you
I see life transpire with you
through me, the scent of lavender sends me back to what
we share
I care as I see you do too
you put actions over words and I can't thank you
enough
Bubbs I hope you're the one because I've never been this
grounded in love before
ropes tied from our cores attaching us creating one
my stomach aches as I lie awake thinking about too
much of the future
for now, I'll lie in the present as I enjoy my present that
is you

DEAR THE ONES & ONLY

A friend like you can truly make a person's day
just the thought of you can bring a smile to my face
thank you for comforting me through the days filled
with pain
your hugs truly melt the negativity away
thank you for being the person I can call a best friend
a sisterly connection I wish would never end
Your presence is truly a present
I thank the Divine for gifting so many souls with your
light
A light that continues to shine ever so bright even if
thunderclouds try to roam the sky
I love you
I hope & pray you continue to grow & be the best you
can be every day
The way you love so big
The way you care so much
The way you always seem to listen
Your ways matter
You matter

and no matter what, my love for you will never shatter
You are an ocean of positivity that just sets people free
don't ever doubt for a second the power you hold
you're the warmth in the cold
you're the light in the dark
you're the peace within the hardest of times
you will forever be missed no matter the distance
Anytime you ever feel lost read this & remind yourself of
your purpose
it's received with much love, much light, & much peace
You are the Universe
A being who was just meant to be
Thank you again for your presence that brings
tranquility
<3

I THANK YOU

Thank you for your participation
All from here is dedication & rejuvenation!
Sending love, light, & peace
Thank you for your time.
Growth is something we all must abide especially with
GOD on our side!